Contents

William Collins' dream of knowledge for all began with the publication of his first book in 1819.
A self-educated mill worker, he not only enriched millions of lives, but also founded a flourishing publishing house.
Today, staying true to this spirit, Collins books are packed with inspiration, innovation and practical expertise.
They place you at the centre of a world of possibility and give you exactly what you need to explore it.

Collins. Freedom to teach.

Published by Collins
An imprint of HarperCollins*Publishers*
The News Building, 1 London Bridge Street, London, SE1 9GF, UK

HarperCollins*Publishers*
Macken House, 39/40 Mayor Street Upper, Dublin 1, DO1 C9W8, Ireland

> Browse the complete Collins catalogue at
> **www.collins.co.uk**

10 9 8 7 6 5 4 3

ISBN 978-0-00-846884-2

British Library Cataloguing-in-Publication Data
A catalogue record for this publication is available from the British Library.

Compiled and written by: Fiona Macgregor
Publisher: Elaine Higgleton
Product manager: Letitia Luff
Commissioning editor: Rachel Houghton
Edited by: Hannah Hirst-Dunton
Editorial management: Oriel Square
Cover designer: Kevin Robbins
Cover illustrations: Jouve India Pvt. Ltd.
Internal illustrations: p 3–10, p 23–28 Priya Kuriyan, p 17–22
Chantelle and Burgen Thorne
Typesetter: Jouve India Pvt. Ltd.
Production controller: Lyndsey Rogers
Printed and bound in the UK using 100% Renewable
Electricity at Martins the Printers

FSC™ C007454 — MIX Paper | Supporting responsible forestry — www.fsc.org

This book is produced from independently certified FSC™ paper to ensure responsible forest management.

For more information visit: www.harpercollins.co.uk/green

Acknowledgements

With thanks to all the kindergarten staff and their schools around the world who have helped with the development of this course, by sharing insights and commenting on and testing sample materials:

Calcutta International School: Sharmila Majumdar, Mrs Pratima Nayar, Preeti Roychoudhury, Tinku Yadav, Lakshmi Khanna, Mousumi Guha, Radhika Dhanuka, Archana Tiwari, Urmita Das; Gateway College (Sri Lanka): Kousala Benedict; Hawar International School: Kareen Barakat, Shahla Mohammed, Jennah Hussain; Manthan International School: Shalini Reddy; Monterey Pre-Primary: Adina Oram; Prometheus School: Aneesha Sahni, Deepa Nanda; Pragyanam School: Monika Sachdev; Rosary Sisters High School: Samar Sabat, Sireen Freij, Hiba Mousa; Solitaire Global School: Devi Nimmagadda; United Charter Schools (UCS): Tabassum Murtaza and staff; Vietnam Australia International School: Holly Simpson

The publishers wish to thank the following for permission to reproduce photographs.

(t = top, c = centre, b = bottom, r = right, l = left)

p 11 michaeljung/Shutterstock, p 12 fizkes/Shutterstock, p 13 Andy Dean Photography/Shutterstock, p 14 Odua Images/Shutterstock, p 15t imtmphoto/Shutterstock, p 15b, p 16 Monkey Business Images/Shutterstock, p 29–31 Will Amlot

Who are you?

I am a baker.

Who are you?

I am a nurse.

Who are you?

I am a scientist.

Who are you?

I am an artist.

Who are you?

I am a bus driver.

Who are you?

I am a dancer.

Who are you?

I am me!

Families

We are two ...

me and you.

We are three ...

Mum, Dad and me.

We are four ...

but maybe more!

We are five ...

off for a drive.

We are five ...

plus one!

Families are different.

Families are fun!

What do you smell, Mirabelle?

Mirabelle, Mirabelle, what do you smell?

Spike, Spike, what does it taste like?

Aneel, Aneel, what do you feel?

Samir, Samir, what do you hear?

Willamee, Willamee, what do you see?

A party!

The rabbits

They are in the cage.

They are out of the cage.

They are in the garden.

They are in the house.

Run, quick!

They are in the cage.

Dig it

Dad picks a pot.

The pots are for plants.

Dad digs a pit.

I put in the plant.

Dad pats the top.

I pat the top too.

Reading notes

Story	Sounds	Language structures
Who are you?	'i', 'a', 'm'	Asking: *Who are you?* Replying: *I am (a)…*
Families	'a', 'm', 'w', 'e'	Counting family members: *We are…* (and the numbers 1–6)
What do you smell, Mirabelle?	's', 'm', 'e'	Identifying what they can see or smell: *I see…*; *I smell…*
The rabbits	'i', 'n', 'c'	Using position words: *It is in the…*
Dig it	'p', 't', 'd', 'n', 'i', 'a'	Making simple words such as *in, dig, pat, dad*

When you read these stories to your children at home, point out the new sound(s) in each story. Encourage your child to find the letter on the page. Then get them to say the sound, and the word, out loud.

Practise these language structures by asking questions. For example, ask: *Who are you?* to elicit the response: *I am a learner*; or ask: *Who is this?* to get the answer: *This is Dad.*